# Tracking the Weather

**Monika Davies**

## Consultant

**Catherine Hollinger, CID, CLIA**
EPA WaterSense Partner
Environmental Consultant

**Image Credits:** Cover & p.1 dmac/Alamy; p.14 Dennis MacDonald/Alamy; pp.5, 26 Ryan McGinnis/Alamy; p.9 RGB Ventures/SuperStock/Alamy; p.27 (bottom) ZUMA Press, Inc./Alamy; pp.10, 18, 25 (Illustrations) Tim Bradley; p.11 Cargo Collective; p.12 Lexa Hoang; backcover, pp.6 (background), 10 (left), 14, 15, 20–23 (background), 21 (top & bottom), 24–25 (background), 31 iStock; p.17 STR/EPA/Newscom; p.4 Getty Images/Science Faction; pp.28–29 (Illustrations) J.J. Rudisill; pp.11, 23 Wikipedia; all other images from Shutterstock.

**Library of Congress Cataloging-in-Publication Data**

Davies, Monika, author.
  Tracking the weather / Monika Davies.
    pages cm
  Summary: "Rain, sunshine, warm fronts, and cold fronts. Have you ever listened to a weather report? Knowing the weather can help us plan ahead. But reporters aren't the only ones who can track weather. You can, too!"
  Audience: K to grade 3.
  Includes index.
  ISBN 978-1-4807-4648-0 (pbk.)
  ISBN 1-4807-4648-7 (pbk.)
  ISBN 978-1-4807-5092-0 (ebook)
  1.  Weather forecasting—Juvenile literature.
  2.  Meteorological instruments—Juvenile literature.
  3.  Weather forecasting—Technique—Juvenile literature.
    I. Title.
  QC995.43.D37 2015
  551.63—dc23
                                                    2014034278

### Teacher Created Materials

5301 Oceanus Drive
Huntington Beach, CA  92649-1030
http://www.tcmpub.com

**ISBN 978-1-4807-4648-0**

# Table of Contents

# Weather Watchers

Have you looked out the window today? Did you notice if the sun was high in the sky? Or did you see dark rain clouds? Was the wind shaking the trees, or was there snow falling?

**Weather** is the state of the air at a certain place and time. The sun may be shining. The air may be hot or cold. The wind may be blowing. Or there may be rain falling. These are all different types of weather. Most weather is mild. But some weather is dangerous. **Meteorologists** track the weather so we can predict and plan for changes.

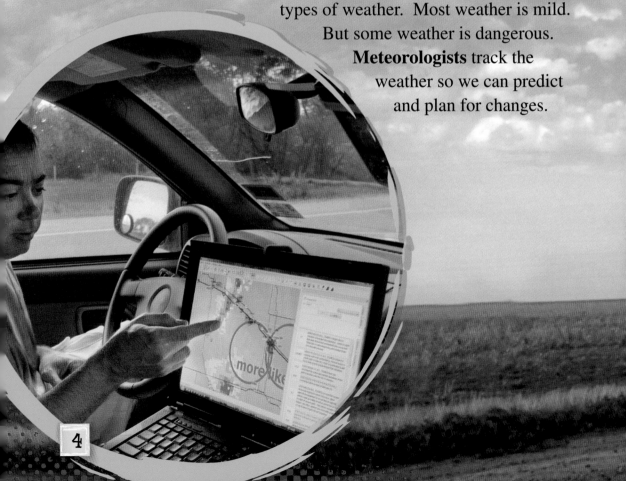

# Storm Chasers

Most meteorologists work inside where they and their computers can stay warm and dry. But some meteorologists race outside to catch a glimpse of the latest storms. It is dangerous, but their work helps us better understand how small changes in the air can produce big changes on the ground.

Weather forecasts can cover national trends, showing expected weather for the country or local areas.

A **forecast** is a prediction of future weather. You can find forecasts in newspapers or online. Simple symbols help readers quickly know what the weather will be. Most forecasts note the high and low **temperatures** expected each day. Checking the forecast can help you prepare for the week. If a storm is coming, you will know to stay inside. If it is going to be sunny, you can plan a day outside.

when

where

weather symbol

temperature in Celsius (C) and Fahrenheit (F)

10:56 PM

**Five–Day Forecast**

NEW YORK CITY

MONDAY

03:21 PM

High 55°F/13°C
Low 23°F/-5°C

Cloudy, rain, and
drizzle into evening

38%

TUESDAY

High 28°F/-2°C
Low 20°F/-7°C

WEDNESDAY

High 46°F/8°C
Low 39°F/4°C

THURSDAY

High 56°F/13°C
Low 36°F/2°C

FRIDAY

High 45°F/7°C
Low 21°F/-6°C

# Modern Measurements

Meteorologists use many tools to make their forecasts. Some tools are new and modern. Other tools have been around for hundreds of years. All of them provide powerful **data** for scientists.

**Satellites** in space take pictures of Earth. They also record data such as wind speed. This information helps experts track weather patterns. These patterns provide clues about weather that is on the way.

**Radar** tells us where there is water in the air. It can show where the water will fall. Radar can determine if the water will be rain, snow, sleet, or hail.

The National Weather Service analyzes billions of data points every day to make its predictions.

## A Stormy Surprise

Powerful computers help forecasters make sense of all the data they collect. But weather is constantly changing. And small changes in the weather in one place can affect other areas. That means, sometimes, forecasters get it wrong—and we get a stormy surprise!

Computers use different colors to show the heaviest areas of rain during a storm.

# Tracking Temperature

The first **thermometer** was built in the late 1500s. But this tool is as important as any modern satellite or radar system. Classic thermometers rely on the fact that liquids take up more space when they are warm and less space when they are cold.

If the air is cold, the liquid in a glass thermometer shrinks. If the air is warm, the liquid expands. The top of the liquid always lines up with a number. This number is the temperature. It tells you how hot or cold it is outside. A high number means the weather is very warm. A low number means it is chilly.

thermometer from the mid-1600s

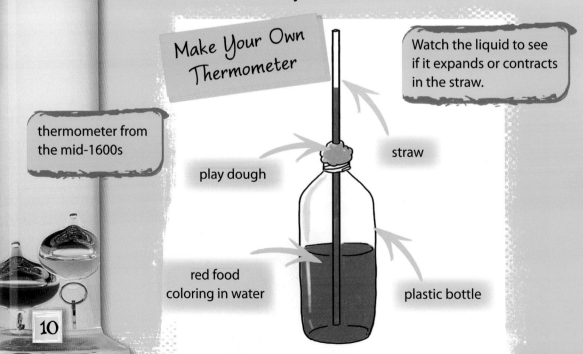

Make Your Own Thermometer

Watch the liquid to see if it expands or contracts in the straw.

straw

play dough

red food coloring in water

plastic bottle

°C °F

50    120

40    100

30    80

20    60

10

0

Anders Celsius

Daniel Fahrenheit

The Greek word *metron* means "measure." This root word can be found in the names of many measurement tools.

## Meaningful Measurements

Temperature is measured in degrees. There are two ways to measure it—Fahrenheit (°F) and Celsius (°C). Fahrenheit is named after Daniel Fahrenheit. Celsius is named after Anders Celsius. Both methods measure the same thing. But they use different scales—100°F is equal to 38°C.

0

20

Scientists track warm and cold fronts in the air. A front is the place where large areas of warm and cold air meet. A cold front occurs where cold air is moving into warm air. It often means rain and thunder are in the forecast. A warm front occurs when warm air moves into a large area of cold air. Warm fronts can cause rain, too. Warm fronts tend to move more slowly than cold fronts.

# Extremes

It can get pretty hot on Earth! The hottest day recorded was 58°C (136°F). It can be chilly here, too. The coldest day recorded was -92°C (-134°F).

cold front

warm front

This scale shows the temperature in degrees Fahrenheit.

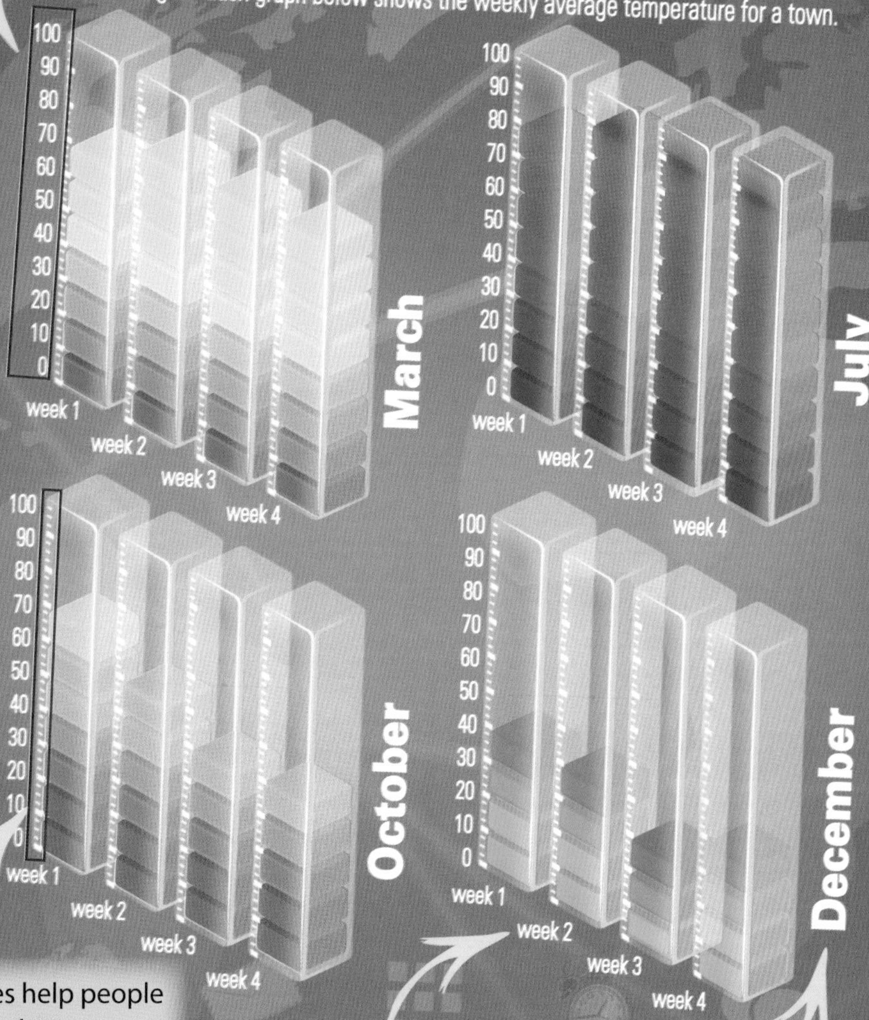

# Seasonal Temperatures

Temperatures change where we live every day. We can use bar graphs to record these changes. Each graph below shows the weekly average temperature for a town.

**March**

week 1
week 2
week 3
week 4

**July**

week 1
week 2
week 3
week 4

**October**

week 1
week 2
week 3
week 4

**December**

week 1
week 2
week 3
week 4

Grid lines help people read the data.

Labels show the category (month) being measured (in weeks).

# Recording the Rain

If you see dark clouds low in the sky, grab your umbrella or run inside. These are stratus clouds, and they are full of rain! A large storm can do more than soak your clothes. It can damage power lines and cause flooding.

Scientists use radar to predict when and where rain will strike. News reports show the path a storm is expected to take. They tell the **probability** of a storm hitting nearby areas.

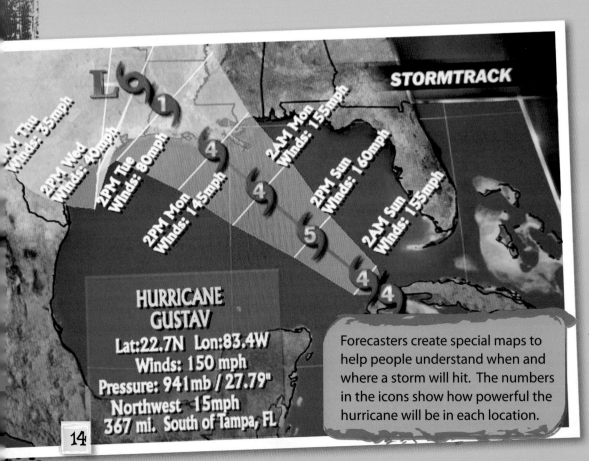

STORMTRACK

2AM Thu Winds: 35mph
2PM Wed Winds: 40mph
2PM Tue Winds: 80mph
2PM Mon Winds: 145mph
2AM Mon Winds: 155mph
2PM Sun Winds: 160mph
2AM Sun Winds: 155mph

**HURRICANE GUSTAV**
Lat:22.7N  Lon:83.4W
Winds: 150 mph
Pressure: 941mb / 27.79"
Northwest  15mph
367 mi. South of Tampa, FL

Forecasters create special maps to help people understand when and where a storm will hit. The numbers in the icons show how powerful the hurricane will be in each location.

# Cloud Chart

Clouds in the sky can provide clues about what the weather will be. There are many types of clouds. These are some of the most common.

Stratus clouds are flat and long. Rain is probably in the forecast when these clouds are low and gray.

Cirrus (SIR-uhs) clouds look like wispy feathers high in the sky. Warm days are most likely ahead when these clouds arrive.

Cumulus clouds are puffy and often low in the sky. They can grow very tall. These clouds can be seen on a sunny day. But, sometimes they produce serious storms.

Clouds are made of tiny water droplets.

Scientists track rain as it approaches. Then, once it arrives, they measure it. A **rain gauge** is an instrument that shows how much rain has fallen. An open container with numbered lines on the side catches rain when it falls. The lines show how much liquid is in the container.

If you want to use a rain gauge during a big storm, place it outside in an open area. Avoid placing it by trees or bushes. (They could affect the amount of water that drops into the gauge.) When the storm is over, the gauge will show how much rain fell from the sky.

## The Raindrop Report

We can track how much rain has fallen with a pictograph. This graph shows one rainy week with sections for each day. Each section has a number of raindrops. A raindrop represents half an inch of rain. Can you tell which day had the most rain? If you said Wednesday, you are right!

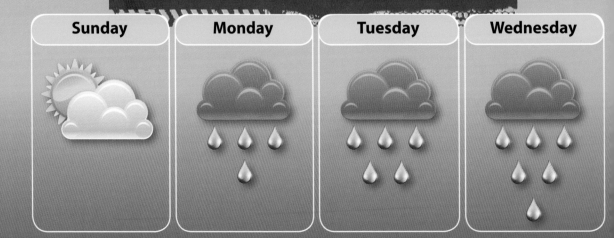

| Sunday | Monday | Tuesday | Wednesday |

rain gauge

Meghalaya, India, receives the most inches of rain per year. The name Meghalaya means "land of the clouds."

| Thursday | Friday | Saturday |
|---|---|---|
|  |  |  |

# Assessing Air Pressure

We may say something is as "light as air." But scientists know air can be heavy. Air in the **atmosphere** pushes down on us all the time, and this pressure has a big effect on weather.

A **barometer** measures air pressure. Barometers are made of a glass tube and are filled with liquid. The bottom of the tube is open and sits inside the cup.

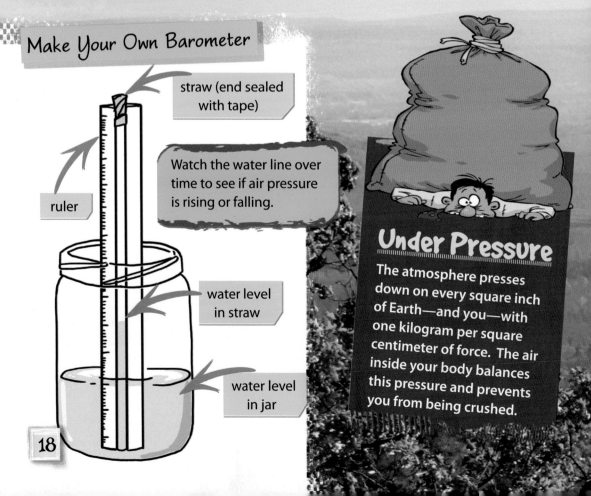

## Make Your Own Barometer

straw (end sealed with tape)

Watch the water line over time to see if air pressure is rising or falling.

ruler

water level in straw

water level in jar

## Under Pressure

The atmosphere presses down on every square inch of Earth—and you—with one kilogram per square centimeter of force. The air inside your body balances this pressure and prevents you from being crushed.

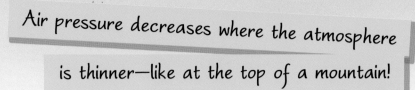

Air pressure decreases where the atmosphere is thinner—like at the top of a mountain!

When air pressure is high, air pushes down on the liquid in the cup. The liquid inside the tube is then pushed up. When air pressure is low, air does not push down as hard. The liquid inside the tube goes down.

Scientists use barometers to measure air pressure. If air pressure is high, air is sinking. When air sinks closer to Earth, it becomes dry. Dry air means there will likely be sunny skies.

If air pressure is low, air is rising. When air rises away from Earth, it changes into clouds and rain. Wet air can cause stormy weather.

Watch your barometer closely. The higher the number, the higher the pressure. If air pressure is high, you will likely see clear skies. If air pressure is low, it may be time to put on your rain boots.

## Furry Forecasters

Have you ever wondered why your dog rushes inside, only to find it is suddenly raining outside a few minutes later? Animals notice and react to changes in air pressure, temperature, and wind very quickly.

barometer

# Watching the Wind

**Wind vanes** show us the direction the wind is blowing. They are often on top of buildings. Wind vanes have four short arrows that point to the north, south, east, and west. These arrows remain still. A longer arrow on top moves with the wind. It points in the direction the wind is blowing. For example, if the pointer is aligned with the north arrow, the wind is blowing northward.

wind vane

Knowing which way the wind blows helps pilots and air traffic controllers decide where the best places are for takeoffs and landings.

# Using a Wind Rose

Scientists use a wind rose chart to track wind patterns. A wind rose chart shows the direction and speed of wind in an area. If a storm is coming, meteorologists know which way the wind will likely blow during the storm.

Darker colors mean the wind is blowing gently. Lighter colors mean the wind is blowing forcefully.

N

N

E

S

**3.6%**

2%
4%
6%
8%
10%
12%

**Wind Speed**
(kilometers per hour)

15.50 (1.6%)

10.80 (6.1%)

8.23 (27.6%)

5.14 (35.0%)

3.09 (22.0%)

1.54 (0.0%)

0.00 (3.6%)

This label shows the direction the wind is blowing.

The percentage shows how often the wind blows at each speed.

While a wind vane shows the direction the wind is blowing, an **anemometer** measures how fast the wind is blowing. This device is made of cups attached to a pole. The harder the wind blows, the faster the cups spin. An anemometer records the number of times the cups go in a full circle. It counts this number over a set period of time. This calculates wind speed.

A change in wind speed could mean a storm is coming. Wind speed can also tell us how fast a storm will move.

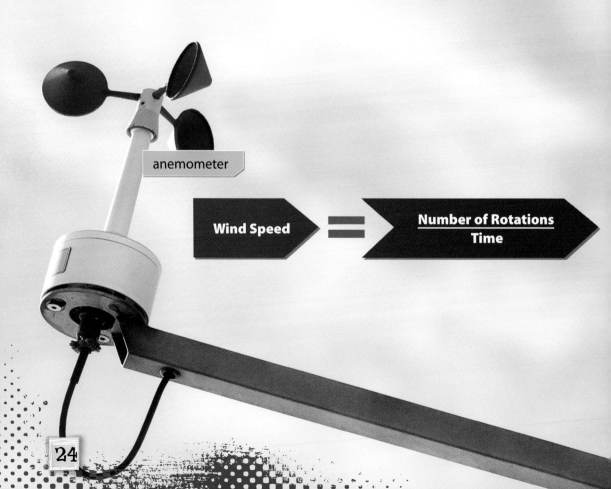

anemometer

Wind Speed = $\dfrac{\text{Number of Rotations}}{\text{Time}}$

The windiest place in the world is in Antarctica.

## Make Your Own Anemometer

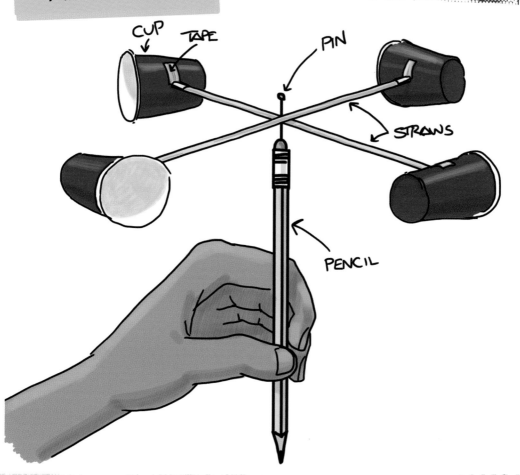

CUP
TAPE
PIN
STRAWS
PENCIL

25

# Power in Numbers

There are patterns in the sky. They may be invisible to the untrained eye. But for those who know what tools to use, weather tells a fascinating story. Meteorologists measure temperature, wind speed, and air pressure. They watch clouds and check for moisture in the air. Day by day, they predict the weather. The work they do informs and protects us. The work they do is never done!

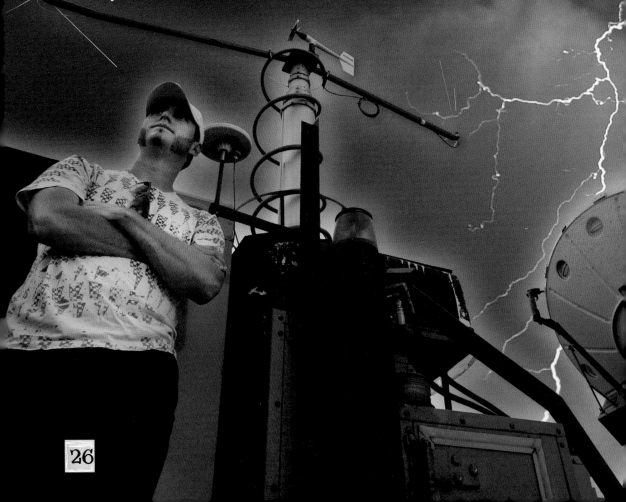

storm damage

volunteer disaster relief

EMERGENCY COMMUNITIES
Presents

"When all is said and done, the weather and love are the two elements about which one can never be sure."
—Alice Hoffman, writer

# Think Like a Scientist

What happens when a cold front meets a warm front? Experiment and find out!

## What to Get

- 2 blue balloons
- 2 large tubs
- 2 red balloons
- cold water
- warm water

# What to Do

**1** Completely fill the red balloons with warm water and the blue balloons with cold water. Make sure there is no air in the balloons.

**2** Fill one large tub with warm water and one large tub with cold water.

**3** Place the balloons in each tub. Observe how the cold and warm liquids interact with each other. Record your observations in a chart like the one below.

Cold Water

Warm Water

**4** Air in the atmosphere behaves the same way. How might that affect weather?

| Cold Balloon+Cold Water | Warm Balloon+Cold Water |
|---|---|
| Cold Balloon+Warm Water | Warm Balloon+Warm Water |

# Glossary

**anemometer**—instrument for measuring the speed and direction of wind

**atmosphere**—the mass of air that surrounds Earth

**barometer**—instrument for measuring air pressure

**data**—information used to calculate, analyze, or plan something

**forecast**—a statement about what you think will happen in the future

**meteorologists**—people who study the atmosphere, weather, and weather forecasting

**probability**—the chance that something will happen

**radar**—a device that uses radio waves to find objects

**rain gauge**—an instrument that shows how much rain has fallen

**satellites**—objects in space that orbit other larger objects

**temperatures**—measurements that tell you how hot or cold something is

**thermometer**—an instrument used to measure temperature

**weather**—the state of the air and atmosphere at a particular time and place

**wind vanes**—devices that show the direction wind is blowing

# Index

# Your Turn!

## Be a Meteorologist

Meteorologists look for patterns. Spend a week studying the relationship between the types of clouds in the sky and air temperature. Each day, draw the clouds—once in the morning and once at night. Record the temperature each time you draw. At the end of the week, review your data. Are there any patterns?